World Languages

Families in German

Daniel Nunn

Raintree is an imprint of Capstone Global Library Limited, a company incorporated in England and Wales having its registered office at 7 Pilgrim Street, London, EC4V 6LB – Registered company number: 6695582

www.raintreepublishers.co.uk
myorders@raintreepublishers.co.uk

Text © Capstone Global Library Limited 2013
First published in hardback in 2013
First published in paperback in 2014
The moral rights of the proprietor have been asserted.

Edited by Daniel Nunn, Rebecca Rissman & Sian Smith
Designed by Joanna Hinton-Malivoire
Picture research by Tracy Cummins
Production by Victoria Fitzgerald
Originated by Capstone Global Library Ltd
Printed and bound in China by Leo Paper Products Ltd

ISBN 978 1 406 25087 9 (hardback)
16 15 14 13 12
10 9 8 7 6 5 4 3 2 1

ISBN 978 1 406 25094 7 (paperback)
17 16 15 14 13
10 9 8 7 6 5 4 3 2 1

British Library Cataloguing in Publication Data
Nunn, Daniel.
Families in German: die Familien. – (World languages. Families)
1. German language–Vocabulary–Pictorial works–Juvenile literature. 2. Families–Germany–Terminology–Pictorial works–Juvenile literature.
I. Title II. Series
438.1-dc23

Acknowledgements

We would like to thank the following for permission to reproduce photographs: Shutterstock pp.4 (Catalin Petolea), 5 (optimarc), 5, 6 (Petrenko Andriy), 5, 7 (Tyler Olson), 5, 8 (Andrey Shadrin), 9 (Erika Cross), 10 (Alena Brozova), 5, 11 (Maxim Petrichuk), 12 (auremar), 13 (Mika Heittola), 5, 14, 15 (Alexander Raths), 5, 16 (Samuel Borges), 17 (Vitalii Nesterchuk), 18 (pat138241), 19 (Fotokostic), 20 (Cheryl Casey), 21 (spotmatik).

Cover photographs of two women and a man reproduced with permission of Shutterstock (Yuri Arcurs). Cover photograph of a girl reproduced with permission of istockphoto (© Sean Lockes). Back cover photograph of a girl reproduced with permission of Shutterstock (Erika Cross).

We would like to thank Regina Irwin for her invaluable help in the preparation of this book.

Every effort has been made to contact copyright holders of material reproduced in this book. Any omissions will be rectified in subsequent printings if notice is given to the publisher.

Contents

Meine Mutter und mein Vater

meine Mutter

Hier ist meine Mutter.

This is my mother.

mein Vater

Hier ist mein Vater.

This is my father.

Meine Cousine und mein Cousin

meine Cousine

Hier sind meine Cousine und mein Cousin.

18 These are my cousins.

21

19

Meine Freunde

meine Freundin

Hier sind meine Freunde.

These are my friends.

Index

Notes for parents and teachers
In German, nouns always begin with a cap

The spelling of the German word for "my" c
on whether it is masculine, feminine, or plu